FINDING FAITH

ANDREW KNOWLES

FINDING FAITH

A LION MANUAL

Copyright © 1983 Lion Publishing

Published by
Lion Publishing plc
Icknield Way, Tring, Herts, England
ISBN 0 85648 363 X
Lion Publishing Corporation
10885 Textile Road, Belleville, Michigan 48111, USA
ISBN 0 85648 363 X
Albatross Books
PO Box 320, Sutherland, NSW 2232, Australia
ISBN 0 86760 382 8

First edition 1983
Reprinted 1984
Reprinted 1985 (twice)
All rights reserved
Printed in Yugoslavia by Mladinska Knjiga

Contents

THE BIG QUESTIONS

Alone under a starry sky or lounging in a dole queue or losing a loved one, sooner or later we will have to ask, and answer, the Big Questions.

WHY AM I?

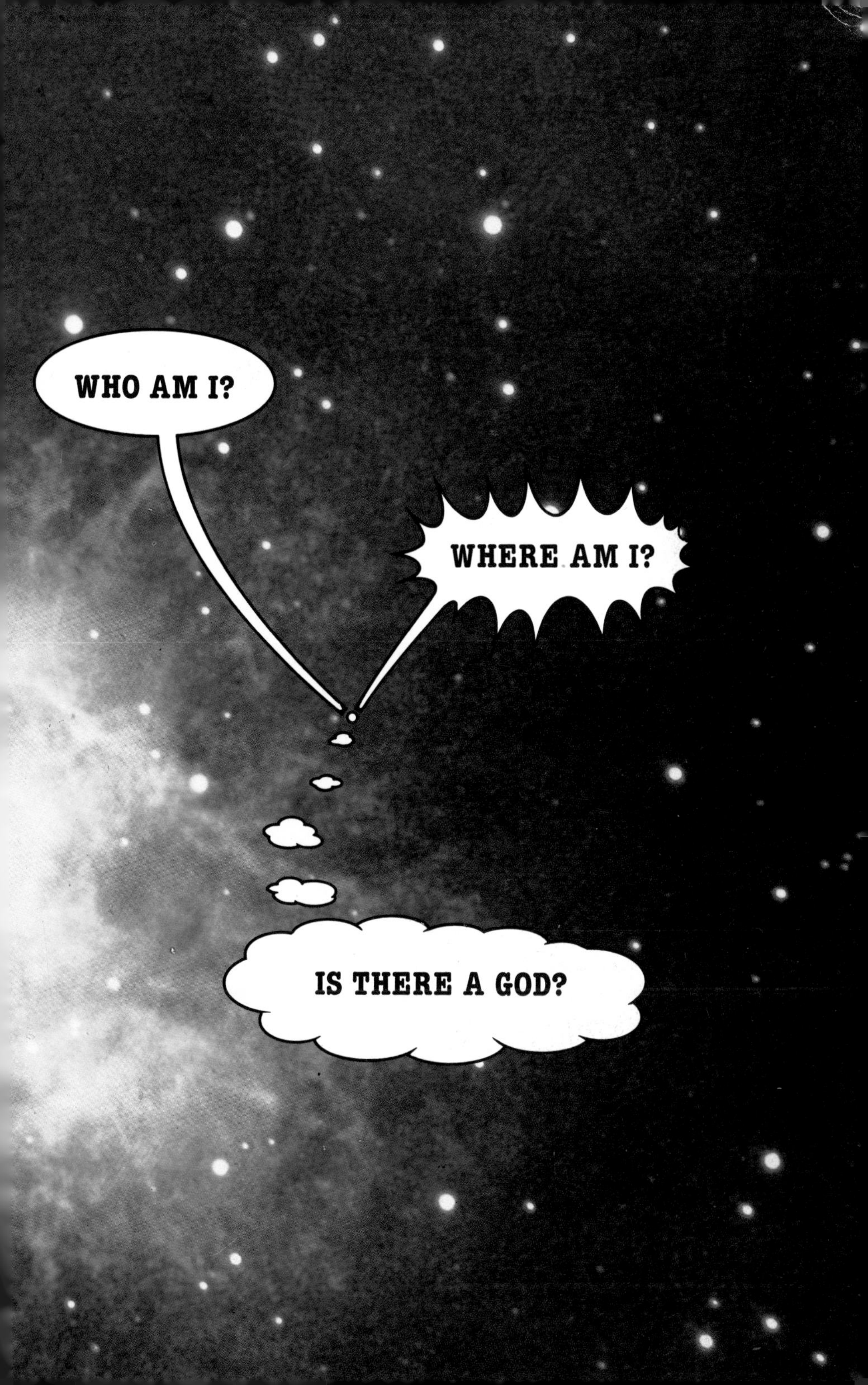
WHO AM I?
WHERE AM I?
IS THERE A GOD?

WHO AM I?

I am a mystery.

I wake up in the morning. I find myself the sole occupant of a complex, sensitive, and extremely useful body. I am also the proud owner of an intricate, imaginative, and highly resourceful brain. Everything about me is unique: my face, my fingerprints, my 'self'.

I am alive. I develop. I grow. So does a vegetable. But I am more than a vegetable. Vegetables don't fall in love, or read the paper, or go on holiday . . .

I am a body with a brain; an animal. But. – I am more than an animal. Animals don't peer through telescopes, or send birthday cards, or play chess, or cook . . .

The chemist tells me I am composed mostly of water, and contain quantities of carbon, calcium, and salt.

The biologist classifies me as Homo sapiens – a species of the sub-family Homininae filed among the Primates . . .

WHERE AM I?

The astronomer tells me I am a speck on the face of a medium-sized planet spinning round a middle-aged star. The star, 'our' sun, is just one of a thousand million million million stars in a universe seventeen thousand million years old.

I feel small. I feel lonely.

WHY AM I?

Am I really a random coincidence, adrift in a cosmic accident, meaning nothing, going nowhere?

Surely I have a dimension that animals and vegetables lack? After all, a carrot is oblivious of the size of Jupiter. A cow cares nothing for the speed of light.

But I am in a different class. I observe and appreciate. I create and choose. I am aware. I criticize Sometimes I even criticize myself!

I am different. I am 'mankind'. In fact the Bible says I am 'Godkind'.

The Bible tells me that I am 'like God'; that I exist in something of the way that God exists, that I am aware in some of the ways that God is aware.

And although I cannot prove it, the idea that I am made in the image of God makes more sense than all the other views put together. Indeed, it helps me to put the other views together, and see them, and myself, as a whole.

**I am a person
created by God
unique in the entire universe
and in the whole of history
and I know it!**

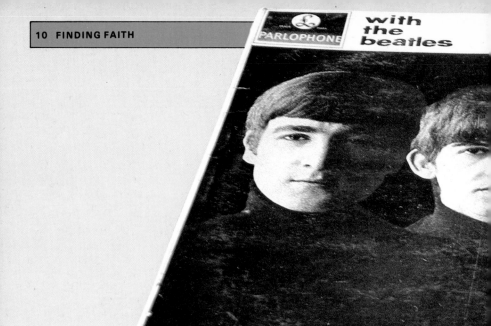

MAN (Homo sapiens) is a species of the sub-family Homininae of the super-family Hominoidea of the sub-order Simiae (or Anthropoidea) of the order Primates of the infra-class Eutheria of the sub-class Theria of the class Mammalia of the sub-phylum Vertebrata (Craniata) of the phylum Chordata of the sub-kingdom Metazoa of the animal kingdom.

Guinness Book of Records

Man is the only animal that blushes – and the only animal that needs to!

Mark Twain

Then God said, 'And now we will make human beings; they will be like us and resemble us. They will have power over the fish, the birds, and all animals, domestic and wild, large and small.' So God created human beings, making them to be like himself.

Genesis 1

Help! I need somebody.
The Beatles

We can control the motions of satellites orbiting distant planets, but cannot control the situation in Northern Ireland. Men can leave the earth and land on the moon, but cannot cross from East to West Berlin.

If thou hearest that a mountain has moved, believe it. But if thou hearest that a man has changed his nature, do not believe it.

I am fearfully and wonderfully made.

Arthur Koestler in Janus.   **The Psalmist**   **Muslim proverb**

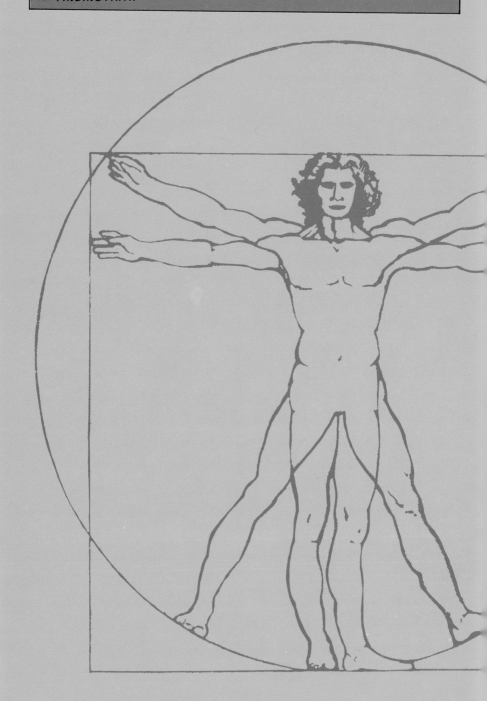

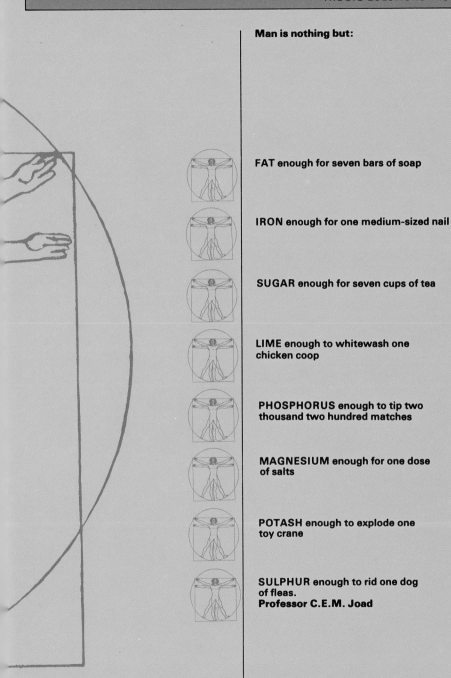

Man is nothing but:

FAT enough for seven bars of soap

IRON enough for one medium-sized nail

SUGAR enough for seven cups of tea

LIME enough to whitewash one chicken coop

PHOSPHORUS enough to tip two thousand two hundred matches

MAGNESIUM enough for one dose of salts

POTASH enough to explode one toy crane

SULPHUR enough to rid one dog of fleas.
Professor C.E.M. Joad

The Frenzied Search for Meaning

Protesters and punk-rockers doing their own thing. Even drop-outs are conformist!

'God is inside you', claims the drug scene.

Eastern promise: Maharish Mahesh Yogi, a physics graduate with a luxurious headquarters in Switzerland, helps his disciples to realize their full potential through transcendental meditation.

Chinese Yarrow stalks (forty-nine of them to be manipulated and interpreted), Tarot cards and Ouija boards are a way in to occult practices for many today.

Mythology: Do ley lines converge at Glastonbury and Stonehenge from sacred sites? Can we plug in to a power grid of natural magic?

Was God a spaceman? Erich von Daniken speculates that superior beings came to earth, mated with apes, built the pyramids and flooded Noah. The Ark of the Covenant was a radio receiver, and the pyramids were deep-freeze chambers for restoring spacemen . . .

Witchcraft appeals to those who don't like their religion too straight.

IS THERE A GOD?

Lots of people believe in God. But are they right?

A Marplan survey in December 1979 found that 82 per cent of the population of Britain have a religious belief of some kind, and 76 per cent said they were Christians. However, only 73 per cent said that they actually believed in God!

When people say they believe in God, they normally mean one of two things:

They have a vague belief that there is a power and purpose behind the universe. Someone or something has set it up, wound it up, and left it to run down. Or

they believe there is some kind of life force that keeps everything going – a deep breathing and steady heart-beat sustaining the cosmos.

Both sets of people would claim to believe in God, but neither would recognize the God of the other! One weaves God into the whole fabric of creation, while the other has a God which is entirely separate, disinterested, and eternally in the distance.

So what can we believe?

It is in fact impossible to prove that God exists through step-by-step argument. If there was such a proof, it would have been discovered long ago, and no one would be in the slightest doubt!

But while there is no knock-down proof that an all-powerful, personal and loving God exists, there are many pointers in that direction. These are some of them:

Most astronomers now accept the theory that the universe had an instant of creation. It came to birth in a vast fireball explosion fifteen or twenty billion years ago. This is commonly known as the 'Big Bang' theory. Now, if there was a Beginning, could it be that there was a Beginner? The opening words of the Bible are: 'In the beginning, God created the universe . . .'

The universe is a place of majestic harmony and breath-taking variety. On our own planet, life is changing and developing all the time. Now if there is Design, could it be that there is a Designer?

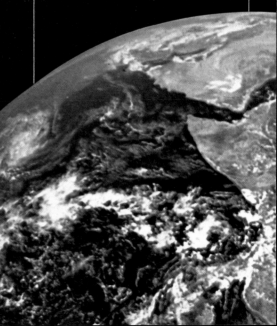

Intelligent life as we know it has come about remarkably 'early' in the history of the universe. The odds against it happening were vast – 'like an explosion in a printing works producing Shakespeare'! Unless, of course, it was intended . . .

Our world has built-in standards. The animal world is guided by instinct, but human beings enjoy free will, balanced by conscience. Why do we value goodness and truth? And how do we account for love? Even those who have never known what it is to love, or be loved, still know they are missing something.

Belief in God

The Christian (and Jewish) belief is that God *does* exist, and that he is a personal Creator. He exists quite independently of his creation, and yet he is intimately involved with it and concerned about it. This means:

The universe is not an accident. It is the work of a supremely powerful, intelligent and creative Being. Indeed, the sheer facts of creation, in all its vastness and variety, are the basic

Creation or accident? Scientists disagree. Equally leading experts in radio astronomy are committed Christians and atheists. Both standpoints require faith. It may take a lot of faith to believe that God created the universe, but perhaps it takes even more to believe that the whole of existence is meaningless chance?

evidence God has given us to show that he exists.

God is personal. It is he who has implanted qualities of goodness and love. The Bible pictures him as like a shepherd, caring for his people at all times and in every way. He is a Father, wanting the very best for his children; respecting their free will, yet providing a moral framework within which they can develop and grow.

ENTER JESUS

a hard-won inner peace. A peace which he could share with others. A peace which was grounded in his complete trust in God his Father. Early in the morning, or late at night, or in the high heat of the day, Jesus would pause for prayer. The result was that, however much he was hassled or interrupted, he never lost sight of who he was, or what he had to do.

And yet, it has to be admitted that there was a most embarrassing side to Jesus. For one thing, he kept company with the dregs of society. He liked nothing better than to dine with known cheats and thieves, and once allowed a prostitute to caress his feet – without even blushing.

He could also be extremely rude. He accused some very distinguished people of play-acting their beliefs and exploiting their status. In fact he told them in no uncertain terms that they stank!

Small wonder the common people heard him gladly.

THE GOSPELS

The story of Jesus is told in four Gospels: Matthew, Mark, Luke and John. They miss out some of the things we would most like to know, such as details of Jesus' appearance – his height, or the colour of his eyes.

Nevertheless, the Gospels provide dozens of episodes showing us how Jesus treated people. We see how he coped with popularity, handled critics, and taught disciples. We witness one interruption after another, as the poor and needy clamour for his help. We trace his steps to Jerusalem, where betrayal, injustice, and crucifixion awaited him.

All the time we hear questions:

'Who is he?'

Who Did Jesus Think He Was?

We know from the accounts of his baptism and temptations that Jesus knew he was none other than God's Son. He had been sent by God on a rescue mission to save mankind from sin and death – a mission which was to cost him his life.

Jesus often called himself the 'Son of Man'. In Jewish scripture, the Son of Man was a divine person in human form. The Jewish hope was that he would come from God to establish an everlasting kingdom, bringing all mankind under God's kingly rule. And this was the title Jesus took to express his calling.

But time and again Jesus warned his disciples, 'The Son of Man must *suffer*.' And so he did. Utterly alone, rejected, and nailed to a wooden cross, Jesus finally brought earth and heaven together. It was through his death that he achieved what his teaching and miracles could never do: he opened a way back to God for lost mankind.

'What right has he?'

'Who do people say that I am?'

'Where does he get it from?'

On one occasion, Jesus asked his disciples for feedback from public opinion:

They told him that people were undecided. Everyone agreed that Jesus was a man of God; a prophet like Elijah. Some thought he might even be John the Baptist, back from the dead. But when Jesus pressed his friends for their personal opinion, Peter had no hesitation in blurting out, 'You are *the Christ*.'

JESUS AS HE WAS

How close can we get to Jesus?

Surely he comes from another world – northern Palestine, two thousand years ago. He never drove a car or caught a bus; never changed a fuse, made a phone call, or spent an evening watching television.

The Gospels show us Jesus as he *was*, and not as we would like him to be. He

was a Jew. As a child he learned the Jewish Law, sitting in the village synagogue-school, reciting it as we would recite nursery rhymes. From his early years, he worked with his father at the carpenter's bench. He knew what it was to get sawdust in his eye, and to patiently fit a yoke to the shoulders of an ox. He was a craftsman.

And the whole atmosphere and pace of his life was so different from ours – the heat of noon, the bleat of sheep, the silence of Sabbath . . .

What was it like to live in that world where only men counted in the synagogue, where women and children were considered relatively unimportant, and where scribes did your reading and writing for you? What was it like to hate Samaritans, and to shake the dust of their country from your clothes? What was it like to be commandeered by a Roman soldier to carry his pack for a mile, or to cross the road to avoid a leper?

This was the world of Jesus. The world in which he worked and worshipped, laughed and cried. And yet he wasn't just the product of his environment.

Take, for example, his attitude to children. He saw something in them which everyone else was missing; a simplicity and trust which God would love to see in adults. Jesus not only observed this for himself, but taught it and lived it out against the grain of public opinion.

He thought for himself. He saw the stupidity of worrying about money: 'How hard it is for a rich man to enter the Kingdom of God.' A daring thing to say in a society that took wealth as a sign of God's blessing!

He saw through the finicky food laws – the endless debate about what was clean and unclean: 'There is nothing that goes into a person from the outside which can make him ritually unclean.'

In other words, food can't make you wicked – it goes straight through you. The wickedness is already there.

In these and many other sayings, Jesus distilled truth into words. Of course, the things he said have been passed down many centuries and across many cultures. They have been translated into the languages of the world. All this has taken them a long way from the mouth of Jesus, who spoke Aramaic with the north-country accent of Galilee. The work of scholars has been to scrape away the grime of the years, so that we can see afresh the words of Jesus in something of their original colour.

When this is done, we come face to face with the amazing Jesus. We catch the impact and urgency of his mission. The Kingdom of God is breaking in on us. The final judgement of the world is near. We see the pettiness of so many of our preoccupations: money, fashion, security and success. We begin to see things the Jesus way.

There are surprises. The parable of the Good Samaritan isn't about doing a good turn every day. The story of the Prodigal Son isn't about juvenile delinquency.

And there is fun. Jesus seems to have found camels as amusing as we do. He gives his disciples nicknames: James and John are 'the MacThunders', and unstable Simon is 'the Rock'. Jesus' laughter must have shattered many a Sabbath stillness – much to the annoyance of the pious neighbours.

Yes, Jesus *is* from another world. A first-century Jew steeped in the life and language of the Palestine of his day. But when we realize what he was saying and doing there and then, we are well on the way to hearing and understanding him for ourselves here and now – today.

Did Jesus Really Happen?

Did the friends and followers of Jesus tell the truth? Did the early writers tell the story the way it was, or did they let their imaginations run away with them?

Was Jesus the son of a virgin?

Did he really defeat death and return from the grave?

Did he turn water to wine at a wedding, feed a multitude from a few loaves and fishes, walk on water, and still a storm?

Did Jesus really happen? His disciples assure us he did.

John, perhaps the closest of them all, who lived to a ripe old age in Ephesus, wrote this: 'We write to you about the Word of life, which has existed from the very beginning. We have heard it, and we have seen it with our eyes; yes, we have seen it, and our hands have touched it. When this life became visible, we saw it . . .'

John and the other disciples were quite convinced that they had seen something take place in their lifetime, before their very eyes, which had opened a whole new relationship between God and men.

In the New Testament we have 'flavour-sealed' accounts of Jesus, written by those eye-witnesses, or by those who knew the eye-witnesses.

St Paul wrote his letters within living memory of the death and resurrection of Jesus.

There were still many people around who could remember those events as readily as some today can remember the Second World War.

Jesus had been the most talked-about Jew of his day. When he arrived in Jerusalem that fateful Passover, the whole city had been alive with speculation as to what would happen. When he was furtively arrested under cover of darkness, rushed through the courts in the early hours of the morning, and dreadfully executed, the entire population was aware of the event. It took place in the full glare of publicity. There were thousands of people who could say, 'It happened. I was there.'

More than that, the Gospels contain the memories of those who were touched most closely of all – Jesus' family and friends. When these people claimed they had seen Jesus gloriously alive after his death, were they telling the truth? Or were they

in fact a team of liars and forgers? As the years went by, many gave their lives, suffering imprisonment and death for the cause. Would they have done so if they had known it was all a hoax? Surely the source of their gladness and courage was that the good news of Jesus was true.

How else can we explain the explosive growth of the church, from a handful of followers? At first they were outnumbered in Judaism alone by 30,000 to 1, yet they had such a quality of life and love and joy that the size of the group quickly multiplied. Before long we hear of the zealous Saul of Tarsus dramatically converted to the Christian faith. He was stopped in his tracks by the reality of the risen Christ. Soon he is dismissing his impeccable Jewish pedigree and qualifications as so much rubbish, compared with the supreme joy of 'knowing Christ'!

All in all, the impact of Jesus is astonishing. He spent only three years in the public eye. Three years in a fairly remote corner of the Roman Empire. He died in his early thirties – half the age of Karl Marx or Chairman Mao, to say nothing of Confucius, Buddha and Muhammad. Yet his life has changed the history of the world, and today 1,000 million people worship him as God.

If there were no such person as Jesus, where did his teaching come from? Which brilliant and original mind coined those memorable phrases: 'do not cast pearls before swine', 'take the plank out of your own eye', 'render to Caesar', 'suffer the children to come unto me' . . .?

And the finest stories the world has ever heard – the Prodigal Son, the Good Samaritan, the Great Supper, and dozens of others – were they written, compiled and distributed by an unknown genius? St Paul, for example, had one of the finest minds the world has ever seen; but he was one for long and tortuous sentences – pithy stories were hardly his speciality!

There is no doubt that in the Gospels we have a collection of sayings and stories which are very distinctive in manner, style and content. They show us the mind of a single, unique teacher. His name is Jesus.

THE THINGS JESUS DID

It was not until Jesus was about thirty that he began his brief ministry; two or three years spent training disciples, preaching, and healing.

Jesus' life was all of a piece.

He did not merely talk about the love and power of the Kingdom of God. He showed it. He lived it. He was the Kingdom of God in person.

He broke all the rules of social etiquette. He dined with devious and dishonest tax collectors.

He was seen in broad daylight talking to a woman who was known for her succession of lovers. He stopped an important conversation to welcome children and give them a hug. He touched lepers – and corpses.

When challenged about the company he kept, Jesus said, 'Healthy people don't need a doctor; sick people do.' He was attracted to those who were ill in mind or body because they were the very people he had come to help. He wanted them to be the first to enjoy the healing and peace of God's Kingdom.

Jesus chose twelve men to share his life. These were his disciples, and they

Tracking the Truth

A fragment of papyrus has been discovered dating from AD 130. It is a piece from the jigsaw of John's Gospel, and it gives us a glimpse of Jesus on trial before Pilate, the Roman Governor. It includes an explicit statement by Jesus concerning his mission in life, as well as a mention of his death:

'Pilate said to them, "Then you yourselves take him and try him according to your law." They replied, "We are not allowed to put anyone to death." (This happened in order to make the words of Jesus come true, the words he used when he indicated the kind of death he would die.)

Pilate went back into the palace and called Jesus. "Are you the King of the Jews?" he asked him.'

And later the fragment continues:

'So Pilate asked him, "Are you a king, then?" Jesus answered, "You say that I am a king. I was born and came into the world for this one purpose, to speak about the truth. Whoever belongs to the truth listens to me."'

It is very hard to account for this fragment if Jesus never existed!

Some people believe that there was such a person as Jesus, and that he was a remarkable man in many ways, but that his followers tended to exaggerate. The difficulty with this view is that even Jesus' enemies agreed that he performed miracles. In the Gospels, the teaching of Jesus and the miracles of Jesus go hand in hand. We can't

have one without the other, however convenient it would be to keep the Sermon on the Mount and discard the stilling of the storm.

Those who say that the facts about Jesus were blown up out of all proportion at a much later date must reckon with the letters of Paul. They are the earliest documents of Christianity, and they contain, full-fledged, the highest possible view of Jesus as the perfect image of God, and the key figure in time and eternity.

were a mixed bunch. They differed from one another in temperament, background and politics. But at the call of Jesus they were prepared to leave home, family and livelihood. At first they listened to his teaching and watched him at work. Later they were to go out in pairs to preach the good news of the Kingdom themselves, and to show God's power in healing and exorcism.

It speaks volumes that Jesus not only united such diverse characters into a team, but that he also allowed them to subject him to the closest scrutiny day in and day out for something like three years.

Miracles happened!

There is no doubt at all that Jesus performed miracles of healing. Even his enemies agreed that he did so, and accused him of sorcery! In fact it is impossible to 'modernise' the story of Jesus by keeping his teaching and throwing away his miracles. The two go together so closely that you cannot have one without the other.

The miracles were a glimpse of the power of God:

Jesus healed all kinds of illness. The blind and deaf, the paralysed and the diseased. People with leprosy, dropsy, haemorrhage, and fever – all were restored to health. On three occasions Jesus even raised the dead to life.

Unlike other wonder-workers, he effected the cures without elaborate ritual or mumbo-jumbo. He would perhaps touch the person he was healing, or take them by the hand. Once he mixed a muddy paste to put on a blind man's eyes, but Jesus was never sensational. He often told the person concerned not to go shouting about what had happened.

Jesus was an exorcist of evil spirits. Confronted by cases of demon-possession, he simply spoke with life-giving authority: 'Be healed', or 'Come out of him!' An army officer recognized that Jesus had the same kind of command over disease and demons as he had over his men.

A handful of miracles were rather like magic. On one occasion, at a wedding, Jesus turned a large quantity of water into a very fine wine – to make a point.

Again, when a large crowd of people overstayed their time listening to him, Jesus fed them all from a few loaves and fishes.

And Lake Galilee was the setting for some extra ordinary events: two record-breaking catches of fish, the stilling of a storm, and the sight of Jesus himself walking on water!

Miracles cannot happen!

There have been many attempts to explain away these events. Perhaps a single youngster reaching for his picnic reminded the rest of the crowd it was lunch-time – and they got out their sandwiches as well? Maybe Jairus' daughter was merely in a coma? Possibly the storm on Galilee did just happen to stop at the moment Jesus spoke, but was it really a coincidence?

Before we make the Gospels a happy hunting-ground for our own pet theories, we have to answer a basic question.

If Jesus was really the Son of God, and the effects of God's power were to be seen when he was around, would such things as the miracles be possible?

It's a big 'if', but the answer is 'yes'. Unless the story of Jesus is all fiction, he clearly did things which cut across the 'laws of nature'.

But without the miracles, the story of Jesus would make very little sense, and be hardly worth the telling.

In all this, three things are worth bearing in mind:

It is unscientific to say 'the miracles could not have happened'. The scientific approach is surely to weigh the evidence and acknowledge the extraordinary circumstances. 'Laws of nature' are no more than 'what usually happens'.

In John's Gospel, the miracles are treated as 'signs'. When he cured blindness, the action was all of a piece with Jesus' description of himself as 'the Light of the World,' and the application that he is the one who gives spiritual light. Again, the feeding of the crowd was far more than the happy sharing of a small boy's lunch. It was a sign that Jesus is 'the Bread of Life', and the food he gives to men's souls.

Jesus could not perform wonders where there was no faith.

Faith in God was always the active ingredient in the healings of Jesus. He told a woman who had squeezed through the crowd to touch his cloak, 'Your faith has made you well.' Many of the healing stories emphasize the faith either of the patient or of those who asked for the cure on his behalf. But where there was no faith, healing was impossible and Jesus was powerless to help.

Jesus Was Not 'Religious'

Although Jesus got on very well with immoral outcasts, he was in constant friction with those who were religious. Religious people can find their security in rules and regulations (which they keep 'religiously'), and which tend to squeeze God out.

The scribes and Pharisees were scrupulous in their religious observance. But, as Mark Twain has observed, 'They were good in the worst sense of the word'! They meticulously gave 10 per cent of their herbs to God, but ignored the greater issues of justice and mercy.

Jesus accused them of 'straining at gnats and swallowing camels'! And in his parable of the Pharisee and the tax collector, he showed that the Pharisee, despite his prize-winning prayer, was merely worshipping himself. It was the tax collector, the religious non-starter, whom God heard and forgave.

THE THINGS JESUS SAID

The first time Jesus preached, he was nearly lynched!

He was speaking in his home synagogue, to the people he had known since boyhood. Luke tells us that he read them a passage from the prophecy of Isaiah:

66 The Spirit of the Lord is upon me, because he has chosen me to bring good news to the poor.

He has sent me to proclaim liberty to the captives and recovery of sight to the blind; to set free the oppressed and announce that the time has come when the Lord will save his people. 99

Jesus, in Luke 4

He then rolled up the scroll, gave it back to the attendant, and sat down. His next words must have dropped like a bombshell. 'This passage of Scripture has come true today, as you heard it being read.' In other words, 'God is doing these things here and now. He is doing them through me!'

When Jesus sensed their scepticism and hostility, he quietly observed that it would be the same for him as it had been for Elijah and Elisha. Both those great prophets of the past had been rejected by their own people.

Within minutes the congregation had hauled him from the synagogue, dragged him to the edge of a precipice, and fully intended to kill him. But such was his authority that he was able to simply walk through the middle of the crowd and go on his way.

The whole episode was typical of the directness of his teaching and the division he was to cause.

Jesus talked constantly about the Kingdom of God.
For him, the Kingdom was no pipe dream. It was already happening. He was not just lecturing on the theory; he was enjoying the practical!

At the heart of the Kingdom was God's love.
God was searching for his people, like a shepherd going after a lost sheep. When even a single stray was found and brought home, the whole community was invited to rejoice. And there was gladness in heaven when a single miserable sinner was rescued and restored.

Jesus described God's search as like that of a woman who lost a coin from her dowry. She would not rest until she had painstakingly swept her dark little house and found it in her dustpan. Again, her success would be an excuse for a celebration with the neighbours.

Or God's love was like that of a father whose son had run away and

squandered a fortune. Yet every day he kept a constant look-out until at last he saw his boy in the distance. Then, without standing on ceremony, he tucked up his robe and ran along the road to sweep the lad into his arms. And this (you will have guessed) was followed by a party!

The lifestyle of the Kingdom is trust in God:

'I tell you not to worry about the food you need to stay alive or about the clothes you need for your body. Life is much more important than food, and the body much more important than clothes.
Look at the crows: they don't sow seeds or gather a harvest;
they don't have store-rooms or barns;
God feeds them!
You are worth so much more than birds!
Can any of you live a bit longer by worrying about it?'
'Look how the wild flowers grow:
They don't work or make clothes for themselves.
But I tell you that not even King Solomon with all his wealth had clothes as beautiful as one of these flowers.
It is God who clothes the wild grass – grass that is here today and gone tomorrow, burnt up in the oven.
Won't he be all the more sure to clothe you?
How little faith you have!'

But the coming of God's Kingdom involved judgement as well.

It was like harvest time, when the crop is taken in. The wheat is stored, but the weeds are destroyed. There will be a home-coming for God's people, but a day of reckoning for his enemies.

It was like fishermen sorting their catch, or a shepherd separating sheep from goats.

It was like a master returning after a long absence and asking his servants how they had managed his property.

Jesus spoke simply. He took the images and episodes of every day and made windows into heaven. When pressed for a ruling on whom you should love (and whom you could therefore hate), Jesus told the story of a wounded traveller who was left for dead by two devout Jews, but rescued and most generously helped by a hated Samaritan. Anyone can love their friends, but the citizens of the Kingdom love their enemies as well.

Confronted by greed, Jesus told the story of a very successful farmer who was planning his retirement. He was very wisely deciding to take things more easily, when he died suddenly in his sleep. By human standards he was very rich, but in God's sight he was an impoverished fool.

The Kingdom of God is sure to win! Some of Jesus' stories captured the irrepressible life of the Kingdom. It might not seem a very promising start – a carpenter rabbi with a handful of followers – but God's victory was absolutely certain.

It was like a tiny mustard seed, scarcely visible to the naked eye, which would grow to be a mighty tree – a landmark and a shelter.

It was like a small amount of yeast in a large barrel of flour. It would quietly get to work until the whole quantity was leavened.

It was like a sower who, despite losing a lot of his precious seed to birds, thistles and drought, would reap a sensational harvest in the end.

The Kingdom Prayer

Jesus heralded a spiritual revolution when he dared to call God 'Abba', which means 'Daddy' or 'dear Father'.

No one before Jesus had addressed God in this way. The Jewish sense of reverence was far too deep. The name of God was too holy to be defiled by human lips, and in the Essene manuscripts (found in the caves of Qumran in 1947) the name of God is too holy even to be written. Four dots replace the word.

Jesus, however, taught his disciples to approach God with the simple trust of a child with a father:

66 Our Father in heaven: May your holy name be honoured; may your Kingdom come; may your will be done on earth as it is in heaven. Give us today the food we need. Forgive us the wrongs we have done, as we forgive the wrongs that others have done to us. Do not bring us to hard testing, but keep us safe from the Evil One. 99

Matthew 6:9-13

A Turn-up for the Book

Jesus turned the values of his day upside-down. Those who count for nothing in this world are highly prized by God. In these sayings, known as 'The Beatitudes', Jesus describes their reward. Matthew has Jesus delivering these words on a hill – rather implying that they are the greatest thing since the giving of the Law on Mount Sinai!

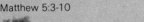

**Happy are those who know they are spiritually poor;
the Kingdom of heaven belongs to them!
Happy are those who mourn;
God will comfort them!
Happy are those who are humble;
they will receive what God has promised!
Happy are those whose greatest desire is to do what
God requires;
God will satisfy them fully!
Happy are those who are merciful to others;
God will be merciful to them!
Happy are the pure in heart;
they will see God!
Happy are those who work for peace;
God will call them his children!
Happy are those who are persecuted because they do
what God requires;
the Kingdom of heaven belongs to them!**

Matthew 5:3-10

JESUS CLAIMED TO BE GOD

The people who heard Jesus were openly astonished at his authority and confidence.

His teaching was peppered with 'It has been said in the past . . . but *I* say . . .', and his frequent 'I tell you' (or 'Take my word for it') was an unmistakable mark of his style.

Not only did he have a very sure touch in handling difficult questions, but he was willing to pit his judgement against time-honoured tradition. He even took issue with the Law of Moses when it came to the question of divorce.

Gradually it became clear, to friend and foe alike, that he was claiming God's authority to a very special degree.

He spoke of himself in a way which included one of the Old Testament names of God, 'I AM':

'I am the bread of life. He who comes to me will never be hungry.'
'I am the light of the world. Whoever follows me will have the light of life and will never walk in darkness.'

And most sensationally of all:

'Before Abraham was born, I AM.'

This was a claim to divinity which was so outrageous that he had to hide in the temple to avoid being stoned on the spot.

Jesus claimed the power and authority of God in other ways. He said he could forgive sins, that he would come in the clouds of heaven, sitting at the right hand of power, and that he could raise the dead.

And to the disciples he said quite simply: 'The Father and I are one.'

Speaking the Truth

Jesus was brilliant at speaking truth to a situation.

When a group of lawyers caught a woman committing adultery (they just happened to be passing?), they challenged him to sentence her to death as prescribed in the Law of Moses. After all, if he pardoned her, he was condoning her immorality.

But Jesus found a third way. He challenged anyone who was innocent to commence the stoning, and the group disappeared. Instead of condemning her to death, Jesus set her free.

But he did not condone her permissiveness. On the contrary, he commanded her not to sin again.

Asked about taxation, Jesus again cut through a complex issue with masterly simplicity.

Was it right for Jews to pay taxes to Rome? If he approved, he was no friend of God's. If he disapproved, he was no friend of Caesar's.

Jesus asked for a Roman coin (which these orthodox Jews just happened to have!). 'Whose image and inscription is this?' he asked. 'Caesar's,' they replied. 'Then give to

Caesar the taxes due to him, and give to God the things that are God's,' said Jesus.

He had refused to be trapped. But by observing that the money bore Caesar's image, he reminded them that people are made in the image of God. And were they giving God his due?

GOD TO THE RESCUE

The story of Jesus is the story of a rescue operation.

Almighty God set out to rescue his creation from futility and death, beginning with mankind. He did it by sending his Son, Jesus. The very name was a declaration of intent, for Jesus means 'God to the rescue'.

So it is that when Mark begins his Gospel, he gives us the happy ending right at the beginning. Despite the fact that a third of his account will be taken up with the depressing facts of Jesus' suffering and death, he is able to say without a shadow of doubt: 'This is the good news about Jesus Christ, the Son of God.'

The first Christians preached that God succeeded in his all-or-nothing rescue mission. And every episode of Jesus' life, from borrowed cradle to empty tomb, is narrated in the light of that victory.

When Jesus was born, angels sang out that God was seeking to make peace with men. Christ's coming was a declaration of war on the kingdom of Satan, not on the human race. For mankind, his coming was a sign of God's overwhelming love, and his irrepressible desire to save. 'God loved the world so much,' says John in his Gospel, 'that he gave his only Son, so that everyone who believes in him may not die but have eternal life.'

All the Gospels speak of the conquest of sin and death through the dying and rising of Jesus. Even so, it was only after the resurrection that it dawned on the disciples what God had been doing all along. At every stage God had been present and active in Jesus. It had all taken place 'before their very eyes'! But only after the resurrection could they see it.

Through Jesus, God had been doing for man what man can never do for himself. He had made a way by which self-centred, proud, disobedient people could be forgiven. It was a way of restoring that friendship with our Maker for which we have been made. And all this not through turning over a new leaf, or trying to be good, but by trusting that Jesus had rescued them.

Every other religion in the world is a DIY job. 'Do it yourself.' 'You can make it if you try.' The Christian faith is something completely different.

New life is God's free gift.

The supplier is Jesus Christ. Good News indeed!

THE HEART OF THE MATTER

THE INESCAPABLE CROSS

The death of Jesus was inevitable. The Jewish leaders engineered it. The Roman soldiers carried it out.

As an exciting and radical teacher, **Jesus had threatened the whole structure of a legalistic religion.** He had exposed the spiritual bankruptcy of the Jewish leaders, and aroused their jealousy.

As a dynamic and popular leader, **he posed a threat to the political order** – the Roman occupiers and their Jewish puppets. Again, his death was inevitable.

But most of all, the death of Jesus was unavoidable because **God intended it.** 'God so loved the world, that he gave his only Son . . .' Jesus himself said, calmly and emphatically, 'No one takes my life from me – I lay it down myself.'

Somehow the hasty execution at Golgotha was at the very heart of God's plan. Jesus himself was born to die, and had repeatedly warned his disciples of the trauma that lay ahead.

The shadow

The cross of Christ has cast a shadow over the history of the world. That single event has made such a radical difference to so many people in so many places over so long a period, that it is quite impossible to imagine the human story without it.

Of course, if Jesus was really the Son of God, there must have been something very deep going on when he died. Again, it was horrible, and mystifying, that such a great and good man was exterminated like a common criminal. If the love of God was on

show as never before, so was the depravity of men.

But the first Christians said their own lives were completely changed by what Jesus did on the cross. Some said their sins had been forgiven through his death. Others said they had found peace of mind, peace with God.

So what had happened?

Jesus made a sacrifice

Sin separates us from God: it can lead only to death.

For centuries, Jews had killed animals. This was to show that they had offended God's holiness deeply and deserved to die. What they did was symbolically to place their guilt on the head of an animal (preferably a prize specimen – the very best of the herd of flock) and then offer its life instead of their own.

The priest would take the animal's blood and pour it on the altar. This was the act of 'atonement'. It showed that the sin which led to death had been dealt with, and that God and the person or people concerned had been reconciled.

But for any thoughtful Jew, it was obvious that more was needed than the repeated slaughter of bullocks and sheep, costly and meaningful as that was. And it was John the Baptist who said when he saw Jesus, 'There is the Lamb of God!' In other words, the death of Jesus (Son of God and perfect man) was the ultimate sacrifice for the waywardness and guilt of the whole human race.

Jesus paid a ransom.

Jesus' own explanation of his death was that he was giving himself as a ransom payment. For us a ransom is the money demanded by kidnappers or terrorist groups as the condition on which they release a prisoner. In Roman times, a ransom was the price paid to secure the freedom of a slave. In fact the slave and the person who was to pay his ransom would take part in a religious ceremony at which the money was paid to the slave's owner in the presence of a pagan god: the idea being that the slave then belonged to the god, and so was a free man.

Jesus took this idea and developed it to show the meaning of his death. His life was a payment to secure the freedom of men and women from the slavery of sin and death. The result was that people had a new owner. They now belonged to God, whose service is perfect freedom.

Jesus went through hell.

The most painful problem of life is the existence of suffering – especially when that suffering is undeserved. If God is loving, and his creation is good, why is there so much heartbreak and misery?

There is no simple answer. Illness, injustice, disease and death, are facts of life in a world spoiled by sin and hostile to God.

Why doesn't God *do* something about it, we cry.

He did.

When Jesus came to this world, he did not excuse himself from suffering. Indeed, on the cross he plumbed the very depths of degradation and despair.

In later years, Peter saw the death of Jesus as an example of how to face and endure injustice: 'When he was

Victory

The cross of Jesus marked the spot where a titanic battle was fought between the love of God and the forces of evil.

Right at the beginning of his ministry, when he was tempted by the devil, Jesus had given Satan notice to quit. By word and deed he had set about releasing men and women from the kingdom of darkness. His whole life had been a sustained onslaught on suffering, sin and death.

On the cross, the world, the flesh and the devil did their worst, and Jesus was apparently defeated.

But God raised his Son from death! The love and justice of God (his love for the world but his hatred of sin), had been completely satisfied and reconciled by the perfect sacrifice of Jesus.

From the death of Jesus onwards, sins can be forgiven and death defeated. The war between good and evil goes on, but the decisive battle has been won.

insulted, he did not answer back . . .
When he suffered, he did not threaten,
but placed his hopes in God, the
righteous Judge.'

Jesus took what was coming to us.
As Jesus died, he shouted at the top of
his voice, **'It is finished!'**

'Finished' was the word Greeks
wrote across bills that had been paid.
On the cross Jesus took our account,
our eternal deficit with God, and met it
in full.

He suffered the disaster and death
that should by rights have been ours,
and we can never even begin to know
what that cost him. He went through
an experience which we thoroughly
deserve but would be unable to bear
and could never survive. Peter again:
'Christ himself carried our sins in his
body to the cross, so that we might die
to sin and live for righteousness. It is by
his wounds that you have been healed.'

THE EASTER FAITH

Jesus' body was put in a rock tomb
on the Friday of Passover weekend. By
Sunday it had vanished. It was a shock
for which the disciples were totally
unprepared. The Jewish authorities
bribed the soldiers who had been
guarding the tomb to say that they had
fallen asleep, and that some followers
of Jesus had seized the corpse.

Did the disciples steal the body?

The accounts in the Gospels show us a
demoralized and frightened group

A hole in history

Quite apart from the
evidence of the Gospels,
there are the facts of
history to reckon with:

The world-wide move-
ment we know as the
Christian church can be
traced back in history to
Palestine in the year AD
30 or thereabouts.

Something happened
after the death of Jesus
which changed his
followers from cowards
to heroes. Within a few
years they had taken the
Good News from
Jerusalem through Asia
Minor to Rome itself.

Would they have carried
the message of resurrec-
tion so convincingly if
they had known it was all
a lie? And would so
many have undergone
martyrdom, as indeed
they did, if they were all
along harbouring the
secret that Jesus was in
fact dead?

And what made the early
Christians change their
day of worship from Sab-
bath (Saturday) to
Sunday? Surely it was
the central fact of the
Easter faith, that Christ
was raised from death on
a Sunday morning.

Millions of people down
the ages have
experienced the pres-
ence and power of the
risen Christ. They would
all echo the words of Sir
Malcolm Sargent:
'Without Christ I cannot
live; with him I cannot
die.'

Something sensational
happened that first
Easter morning.
Something which left a
hole in history. A hole
the size and shape of the
resurrection of Jesus.

of men. The tomb was guarded. They certainly had no leader capable of planning and carrying out a raid on the tomb.

Did the authorities, Jewish or Roman, intervene?

For the Roman Governor, the unsavoury episode was already closed. But if the priests had managed to persuade him to change the burial place, surely they would have silenced the disciples by producing the remains? The fact that neither side knew the whereabouts of the body is a most exciting and significant aspect of the evidence.

Jesus began to appear to his disciples.

Mary of Magdala was the first to see him. According to John's Gospel, she was weeping at the empty tomb, deeply grieving the death of her master, and angry and frustrated that his body had not been allowed to rest in peace. When the risen Jesus appeared to her, the writer tells us with disarming frankness that, through her tears, she thought she saw the gardener! Anyone forging a legend would hardly include such a detail, and would probably not choose a reformed prostitute as the first witness.

Later the same day, Jesus joined two of the disciples as they walked home to their village. This time Luke tells the story and again every observation rings true. They don't immediately recognize Jesus (though their hearts are strangely warmed when he explains scripture to them). But after they have invited him to their home and he breaks bread with them, it suddenly dawns on them who he is.

Had Jesus merely 'revived'?

Perhaps Jesus had never really died, but only fainted from loss of blood? Maybe he felt better after lying in the cool tomb, and eventually managed to break out?

But this theory ignores the fact that the Romans had double-checked his death. A soldier had pierced Jesus' side, to ensure he was dead. And would a brutally beaten and crucified man recover sufficiently to roll the stone from the mouth of the tomb, overcome the guards, and walk miles on wounded feet? Even had he done so, Jesus would hardly have cut a dash as the Prince of Life!

Were the disciples having hallucinations?

Everything we know of the resurrection indicates that it took the disciples entirely by surprise. The last person they expected to see was Jesus.

Perhaps Mary of Magdala was sufficiently highly-strung to think she had seen a ghost. But she was not the only witness. The risen Christ was seen by Matthew, the hard-headed tax collector, Peter the rugged fisherman, and Thomas the sceptic. On one occasion, 500 people all claimed to have seen Jesus of Nazareth gloriously alive after his death on the cross.

Nor were these appearances all in the eerie light of dawn or suggestive twilight. They happened at all sorts of times and places, and to a wide variety of people.

Jesus had been raised from death.

Gradually a profound conviction settled over the little group of disciples. Jesus had done more than survive crucifixion. He was no pale invalid slowly recuperating from a dreadful ordeal. He was gloriously alive!

Nor was he a vague ghost. He could be clearly seen and distinctly heard. He could be touched. He could eat. And yet he was the same Jesus they had seen hanging on the cross. The marks of his suffering could still be seen and felt.

Somehow he was now the other side of death. God had raised his Son from the grave. And now Jesus had a resurrection body: a spiritual body, mysteriously different, but recognisably the same.

SO WHAT?

What does the resurrection mean for us today?

It means Jesus was who he said he was.

St Paul wrote his first letter to the Christians at Corinth in about AD55. In it he reminds his readers what he had told them round about AD49.

66 **I passed on to you what I received, which is of the greatest importance: that Christ died for our sins, as written in the Scriptures; that he was buried and that he was raised to life three days later, as written in the Scriptures; that he appeared to Peter and then to all twelve apostles. Then he appeared to more than five hundred of his followers at once, most of whom are still alive, although some have died. Then he appeared to James, and afterwards to all the apostles.** 99

Paul, in 1 Corinthians 15

Here we have the roots of the Christian faith: the Jesus facts carefully passed on by word of mouth from the eye-witnesses, the apostles. Paul had checked the story with them just a few years after the crucifixion and resurrection. He had found their evidence totally convincing, and knew of hundreds of other witnesses who were still alive to tell the tale.

It was the resurrection which proved that Jesus was the Christ. Without it there would be no Jesus Christ and no Christianity.

Jesus has made a way back to God.

When Jesus died, he shouted 'It is finished!' A sacrifice had been provided for the guilt and aggro and spite of the human race. The death penalty had been paid in full. Jesus had taken on himself the sin which separates man from God.

Putting it the other way, St Paul writes bluntly: 'And if Christ has not been raised, then your faith is a delusion and you are still lost in your sins.' And he adds that if such is the case, 'we deserve more pity than anyone else in the world'!

The new life of Jesus is the guarantee of our own new life.

Jesus was not raised from death so that he could enjoy eternity in splendid isolation. He said to his disciples, 'Because I live, you shall live too.' Paul calls Jesus 'the prototype' – the first of many. Jesus has bridged the gap between God and man, so that all who trust him can safely cross the gulf of death.

And resurrection starts now!

Because Jesus is alive, we can enjoy his presence today. He is our contemporary Saviour and Lord. As Paul wrote in a rare burst of journalese, 'Man in Christ, New Creature!' For himself he could say with all his heart, 'It is no longer I who live, but Christ who lives in me.'

Ascension

Jesus appeared to his disciples many times after his resurrection. It was as though he was in a state of 'overlap' between earth and heaven. He was able to come and go, teaching his disciples, and assuring them beyond a shadow of doubt that he was alive again.

This went on for about six weeks. At the end of that time, Jesus told his disciples to wait in Jerusalem until they received the Holy Spirit. The Spirit would fill them with power, and enable them to spread the Good News not only in Jerusalem, but to the surrounding areas, and indeed to the ends of the earth.

Then Jesus was received into heaven, and they saw him no more.

Luke, a careful historian, describes what happened when Jesus parted from his disciples for the last time:

'After saying this, Jesus was taken up to heaven as they watched him, and a cloud hid him from their sight.

'They still had their eyes fixed on the sky as he went away, when two men dressed in white suddenly stood beside them and said, "Galileans, why are you standing there looking up at the sky? This Jesus, who was taken from you into heaven, will come back in the same way that you saw him go to heaven." '

Jesus visibly left his disciples and the earth and returned to heaven. He was received back into his father's presence, and resumed the glory which is rightfully his.

Just as he was God's representative on earth, he is now man's representative in heaven. Heaven is where God is. It is 'higher' than earth, not in the sense of being 'above the bright blue sky', but in the sense of being a perfectly harmonious realm of the spirit.

Jesus, in passing into that realm, has secured free and confident access to the presence of God for all who follow him.

4

GOD'S CHOSEN RABBLE

THE CHURCH HAS LIFT-OFF

T he Christian faith burst on an unsuspecting world at nine o'clock on a Sunday morning, probably in the year 30 AD.

The place was Jerusalem, and the occasion was the Jewish festival of Pentecost.

Jesus had told the disciples to wait in Jerusalem for the coming of his spirit. Suddenly, while they were in prayer, the promised gift was given.

Luke describes the coming of the Spirit as 'like a strong wind blowing', and 'like tongues of fire'. The believers were filled with an invisible, burning power, which was none other than the close presence of God.

And they began to speak in foreign languages! Pilgrims who had come from all over the known world were astonished to hear these peasants from Galilee praising God in the tongues and dialects of home. God was giving the spread of the gospel a flying start.

It was Peter who preached. With the support and consent of the other disciples, he made the ringing claim that Jesus had risen from the grave. And this in Jerusalem, within two months of the crucifixion, and within two miles of the tomb.

> 'In accordance with his own plan God had already decided that Jesus would be handed over to you; and you killed him by letting sinful men crucify him. But God raised him from death!'

That day the nucleus of one hundred and twenty believers was expanded by three thousand converts!

THE JESUS PEOPLE

The early church was unstoppable.
It began with the preaching of the
apostles in Jerusalem. When arrested
and threatened with imprisonment and
death, they argued their case with even
greater vigour! Their message was that
Jesus was the promised deliverer, the
Messiah, and that all should turn to
him for forgiveness and new life with
God.

The good news was further
commended by the remarkable warmth
and genuineness of friendship among
the believers. They shared their
belongings, helped those in need, and
met every day to worship in the temple
or enjoy meals in each other's homes.

There was a contagious gladness
about the group, and their numbers
quickly increased.

At first the membership was
exclusively Jewish, but before long it
became clear that the Christian
butterfly was to leave its Hebrew
cocoon. One after another, barriers and
prejudices were broken down.

For example, the church in Jerusalem
was shocked when Samaritans came to
faith in Jesus. Two apostles, Peter and
John rushed over to see for themselves,
welcomed them in Christ, and helped
them receive the Holy Spirit.

An African was converted and baptized
on his way home to Ethiopia.
Saul of Tarsus, the church's cruellest
persecutor, was dramatically converted
on the Damascus road, and became the
apostle Paul.

Peter surprised himself and everyone
else by going into the home of
Cornelius, an officer in the occupying

Roman army. It was a momentous event, taking the new faith not just to Jews or Jewish sympathizers, but to non-Jews, called 'Gentiles'.

Inevitably, the church in Jerusalem was persecuted. But this had the unexpected benefit that the believers were scattered over a wider area, and wherever they went they talked about Jesus. The gospel was 'gossiped' just as much as it was 'preached'.

Before long a fascinating church was established in the cosmopolitan city of Antioch. Second only to Rome, Antioch provided the ideal spring-board into Asia Minor. From there Paul and his team of missionaries pioneered Christianity throughout the Graeco-Roman world.

> **❝ The group of believers was one in mind and heart. No one said that any of his belongings was his own, but they all shared with one another everything they had. With great power the apostles gave witness to the resurrection of the Lord Jesus, and God poured rich blessings on them all. ❞**
>
> Acts 4

Things They Said About Jesus

'The Christ', 'Messiah', 'God's Chosen One' – these were the titles given to Jesus by his followers.

After the resurrection, even doubting Thomas fell on his knees and declared in awe, 'My Lord and my God!' There in the upper room, Jesus accepted the kind of worship which Jews reserved for God alone.

It was not that Jesus had *become* the Son of God. The truth was that he had always existed, independent of time and space.

In John's Gospel Jesus is called 'the Word':

'Before the world was created, the Word already existed; he was with God, and he was the same as God.'

The Word was active in the creation of the universe. The Word was the source of life. Taking up the same theme, Paul wrote that Jesus was 'the visible likeness of the invisible God'. The whole of God was present in Jesus, and it is through him that the creation hangs together. Without him there would be disintegration and chaos.

So what happened when God became a man? Was he merely pretending to be human? Paul explains:

'He (Jesus) always had the nature of God, but he did not think that by force he should try to become equal with God. Instead of this, of his own free will he gave up all he had,

and took the form of a servant.
He became like man and appeared in human likeness.
He was humble and walked the path of obedience all the way to death – his death on the cross.
For this reason God raised him to the highest place above and gave him the name that is greater than any other name.
And so, in honour of the name of Jesus all beings in heaven, on earth, and in the world below will fall on their knees, and all will openly proclaim that Jesus Christ is Lord, to the glory of God the Father.'
Philippians 2:6–11.

Paul

Paul was a small man with a bald head and bandy legs. At least, that's one description of him which has survived the centuries.

We know from his own writings that he had no great natural presence. He was an unimpressive speaker, and he suffered from what he called a 'thorn in the flesh' – which may have been a form of epilepsy.

Born Saul of Tarsus, he grew up in Turkey which had long been part of the Greek world. His family were Jews, and his father had the status of a Roman citizen. A Roman citizen with a Greek mind and a Jewish heart, Paul was uniquely qualified to bridge the gap between Jews and Gentiles.

As a young man, Saul travelled to Jerusalem to train as a rabbi. There he was incensed by the followers of 'The Way' – a new heresy which claimed that Jesus of Nazareth was Messiah. Once qualified, he set about persecuting them with a will.

He was in full flight, heading for the believers in Damascus with threats of murder on his lips, when he had a blinding vision of the risen Christ. In the most famous turnabout of history, Saul of Tarsus was converted to Christianity. In due course he became Paul the apostle, perhaps the brightest jewel in the early church's crown.

It is impossible to over-estimate the part played by Paul in the spread of the Christian faith.

In the course of three epic journeys, he was imprisoned, whipped, stoned and shipwrecked. In city after city he contacted the little Jewish communities, and told them the good news of Jesus the Messiah. He himself counted his impeccable Jewish pedigree as 'so much rubbish' once he had breathed the freedom and love of Christ. If the folk in the synagogues rejected him, he would declare: 'My conscience is clear; now I shall go to the Gentiles.'

Starting from Antioch (where the nickname 'Christians' originated), Paul first took the gospel to Cyprus and Asia Minor, planting churches

in a number of centres.

On his second journey, he consolidated the existing work, and then crossed over to Europe, where he worked in Philippi and Athens. Flogged by Jews, imprisoned by Romans, and taunted by Greeks, he never gave up.

Finally, he was arrested while on a visit to Jerusalem. As a Roman citizen, he was entitled to appeal to Caesar and this he did. The voyage to Rome nearly ended in disaster when the ship was wrecked on the coast of Malta. When he finally arrived in Rome, he was placed under house arrest.

Paul is last heard of in the Bible awaiting trial in Rome. The story goes that he was eventually executed during the vicious persecution of Christians by the Emperor Nero.

Paul's letters, often written from prison, are the earliest writings in the New Testament. They give a vivid picture of Paul himself and the problems he faced.

We glimpse the early church, warts and all: pride, jealousy and backbiting at Corinth; tight-lipped and insensitive legalism among the churches of Galatia. And then there were the questions:

If Christ made you free, were you free to be immoral?

Did non-Jews who became Christians have to take on board the burden of the Jewish Law, including circumcision?

Time and again we see Paul rescuing the infant Christian faith from Jewish attempts to strangle it with legalism, or Gentile attempts to suffocate it by shrouding it in mystery.

It was largely thanks to Paul that the gospel survived and began to break down racial, cultural and social barriers. In his own words:

'There is no longer any distinction between Gentiles and Jews, circumcised and uncircumcised, barbarians, savages, slaves, and free men, but Christ is all, Christ is in all. You are the people of God; he loved you and chose you for his own.'

NEW LIFE — NEW LIFESTYLE

The early Christians had a quality of life and lifestyle which marked them out as followers of Jesus.

They had a 'one-anotherness' among themselves; a committed love which put Christ and others before self. They went beyond all known bounds of behaviour by forgiving their enemies and praying for those who so bitterly persecuted them.

They had an infectious joy and praise, and displayed a simple trust in God and peace of mind even when they were under attack. Not many of them were wealthy, yet they showed an unfailing generosity to the poor and needy. Not many were clever, yet they lived by standards of honesty and truth which shook the pagan world in which they lived, and gave an authentic ring to their message.

Such was the quality of their love that a new Greek word had to be found to describe it. That word was *agape*, selfless love. The world had never seen anything like it. Agape was the hallmark of the Jesus Revolution, and all an outsider could say was, 'See how these Christians love one another!'

Of course the church was far from perfect. There were misunderstandings and mistakes, and no doubt the groups of believers had more than their share of frauds and fanatics. But in spite of everything, including persecution, the simple love and truth of this new society was to conquer the Roman Empire and win the world.

Signs of Membership

Two simple ceremonies have always been part of the life of the church in every age and place. They are Baptism and Holy Communion.

Baptism is a drenching in water which represents at best a wash and at worst a drowning! As a wash, it was a sign that the believer was turning to God for cleansing in the name of Christ, and making a new start in life. As a mini-drowning, it was a sign that the believer was dying to his old life and emerging again to the new life of Jesus.

It was a familiar sign to Jews, who circumcized male converts and baptised women. They also counted children of believing parents as part of the family of faith until they were old enough to understand for themselves.

John the Baptist had caused a sensation by baptising men and women who had been committed to Judaism all their lives. For John, baptism was a sign of 'repentance' – a change of mind about God, and a new readiness to serve him.

Jesus commanded his disciples to 'go to all peoples everywhere and make them my disciples: baptise them in the name of the Father, the Son, and the Holy Spirit . . .' Ever since, water baptism has been the sign by which the Christian church has marked and welcomed those who have newly come to faith in Christ.

Holy Communion (which is also known as the Mass, the Eucharist, and the Lord's Supper) is a simple meal through which Christians remember the death and resurrection of Christ. On the night of his arrest, Jesus had broken some bread and given it to each of his disciples, with the words, 'This is my body, which is for you. Do this in memory of me.' At the end of the meal (which was probably a Passover celebration) Jesus took a cup of wine and said, 'This cup is God's new covenant, sealed with my blood. Whenever you drink it, do so in memory of me.'

So Christians have always shared in broken bread and poured out wine, just as they share in the fact that Jesus' body was broken on the cross and his blood shed for the sins of the world. This sharing, or 'fellowship', is both with the risen Jesus and with each other. It is a sharing of a common life, a new life made possible by the death and resurrection of Jesus.

Both Baptism and Communion are known as 'sacraments' – visible reminders of God at work. Just as a wedding ring is far more than a band of gold (it represents a married life of unending love); so Baptism and Communion are more than a wash and a meal. They mark the beginning and the continuation of the Christian life.

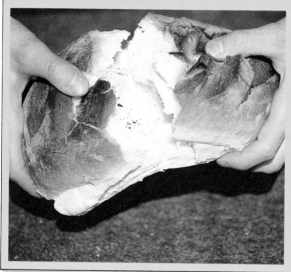

Handing Down the Truth

Wherever Christians gather, they remember that on a certain night their Founder said and did certain things. On that same night he was arrested by his enemies and put on trial. The following day he was executed by crucifixion.

This memory, handed down from one generation to the next, can be traced back to Palestine in the years when Pontius Pilate was the Roman Governor. It may even be that the day of crucifixion, the first Good Friday, can be dated precisely as April AD 30. And whenever the story of Jesus was told, it was noticeable that it was his death which was so significant. His parables had been brilliant and his miracles amazing, but they faded into insignificance when

Passover

compared with the drama of the cross.

We glimpse the living chain of memory within the church in a letter written by a French bishop, Irenaeus, who died at Lyons about the year AD 200. Writing to an old friend, Florinus, he recalls their student days in Asia Minor, when they attended the lectures of Bishop Polycarp. Polycarp (who had died in AD 155 when he was well into his eighties) used to tell them stories about 'John the disciple of the Lord' whom he had known personally many years before.

So when Irenaeus celebrated Communion with fellow-Christians in Lyons, he was passing on something he had been told by his old teacher, whose friend had been there when it happened!

Jewish Passover and Christian Communion are closely linked.

On the night of their deliverance from slavery in Egypt, each Israelite family killed a perfect lamb and daubed its blood on the outside door of the house. That night the Angel of Death swept through Egypt, and the eldest sons of the Egyptians died. But when the angel saw the blood on the doors of the Israelites' homes, he 'passed over' the household, and they escaped the judgement which was falling on the land.

The Passover meal became an annual event for Jewish families, and continues to this day.

When Jesus came, he saw himself in terms of the Passover lamb. It was his life, freely offered, which would be the complete sacrifice for sin, and the means by which a new exodus could take place. The first exodus had been from slavery in Egypt to freedom in the promised land. The new exodus would spring mankind from the prison of sin and death and provide a new life in the family of God.

Christian Leadership

The church has organized itself in a variety of ways over the centuries. Jesus, of course, had trained and commissioned the apostles. Their prime responsibility was to be witnesses to the truth about Jesus. After all, they were the ones who had shared his life, seen his death, and met him alive after his resurrection.

But the apostles were joined by others: deacons who handled administration, prophets who spoke God's word with startling insight, and teachers who deepened people's understanding of the faith.

When Paul wrote to the Christians at Ephesus, he listed the various departments of church leadership: 'apostles, prophets, evangelists, pastors and teachers'. In each case, these were functions for which people had been equipped by the Spirit of God. Spiritual gifts were always for the benefit of others, and never for personal prestige.

Another thought-provoking aspect of the New Testament church was the absence of any professional clergy! There was no need now for sacrifices, so no need for a priesthood to represent people to God. Everyone was a priest! And every member of the Christian family had a part to play, a service to give, and gifts to contribute. The bad old days of overactive priests and passive congregations were still in the future!

5
READ ALL ABOUT IT

THE BIBLE

Christians believe that God has made himself known in various ways:

In creation
The wonders of creation are evidence that there has been a Maker at work. 'How clearly the sky reveals God's glory!' exclaims one of the Psalms; and Paul adds in his letter to the Christians at Rome: 'Ever since God created the world, his invisible qualities, both his eternal power and his divine nature, have been clearly seen; they are perceived in the things that God has made.'

In Scripture
But Christians believe God has shown himself more clearly still in the pages of the Bible. Here we build up a detailed picture of the mind, will and character of the living God; a picture we could never complete from the evidence of creation alone.

The Bible reveals God at work in history, and particularly in his dealings with Israel, the 'chosen people'.

Messages of God's love and anger were delivered at point-blank range by Israel's prophets. Their characteristic phrase, 'the Lord says', sounds like a trumpet through the pages of the Old Testament.

The Old Testament is the first, and larger, section of the Bible. It is really a mini-library of 39 books, including law, history, poetry, prophecy, and practical advice.

The New Testament contains 27 books, including four different accounts of the life of Jesus (the Gospels), an account of the birth and growth of the church (the Acts of the Apostles), several letters (most of them written by Paul), and the Revelation of John.

While the Old Testament books were written by a number of authors over a period of about a thousand years, the New Testament books were all written within living memory of the death and resurrection of Jesus. In other words, they are all-important eye-witness, or first-generation, accounts of what happened.

The Torah: God's Life-line

The Jews' most precious possession was, and is, the Torah; the loving Law of God.

The Psalmist delighted in it, like a dog with a bone.

Even today, when a Jewish teacher comes to the end of the Books of the Law (the first five books of the Bible), he reads the opening words of Genesis, to show that he begins all over again.

The Law is God's own instruction on how to live in the world he has made. Obedience to the Law spells health and wealth, long life and good days.

Israel, remember this! The Lord — and the Lord alone — is our God.
Love the Lord your God with all your heart, with all your soul, and with all your strength.
Never forget these commands that I am giving you today.
Teach them to your children.
Repeat them when you are at home and when you are away, when you are resting and when you are working.
Tie them on your arms and wear them on your foreheads as a reminder.
Write them on the doorposts of your houses and on your gates.

Deuteronomy 6:4-9

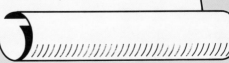

THE GOD WHO MAKES PROMISES

The story of the Jewish nation began with a promise.

God promised a man called Abram that he would be the father of a great people, a nation, and that they would have a land of their own. God's plan was to so guide and bless Abram's descendants, that the world would be able to see the kind of God he is.

The promise God made to Abram was known as the 'covenant', and has always been the corner-stone of the Jewish experience. It was renewed with each successive generation. Abram was given a new name, Abraham. In his old age, he and his wife had a son, Isaac. Isaac had two sons, Esau and Jacob.

God's purpose frequently seemed to hang by a thread. Not only was Isaac born to a very elderly mother, but he was also nearly sacrificed as a child!

Jacob, as the younger son, did not qualify to inherit God's promise to his father. In fact he obtained Isaac's blessing by pretending to be his brother Esau, and deceiving the old man who was sitting in a dark tent and was nearly blind anyway. Despite this rather shaky start, it was to Jacob that God gave the new Israel, and from him that the Israelites traced their descent.

At first sight, God's promise was never fulfilled. Certainly Abraham didn't live to see it. On his death, he had only one true son (hardly a nation!), and a small burial ground (scarcely the promised land!)

The same was true for Isaac and Jacob. Although they pastured their flocks in Palestine, they in no way possessed it. By the standards of their day, they were rootless, powerless, and ignorant.

Had God forgotten his promises, or failed to keep his word?

The descendants of Israel trusted that he had done nothing of the sort. God was utterly faithful, and his promises would stand for all eternity. Therefore it was only a matter of time before the hopes raised in the hearts of their forefathers would be fulfilled.

Covenant

There are a number of covenants in the Old Testament, of which three are especially important:

The covenant with Abraham, by which God promised to give him the land of Canaan.

The covenant with the Israelites, when God promised them, through Moses, that they would be his Chosen People.

The covenant with David, when God promised him that he would always have descendants, and that his kingdom would last for ever.

A covenant was sometimes in the nature of a bargain. When God committed himself to the people of Israel, for example, he promised to look after them and protect them. They were his subjects, and he their Lord. At the same time, the people had to give their undivided loyalty to God, and keep his laws.

But when God made his covenants with Abraham and David, there were *no conditions* to be met by the men concerned. God had somehow set his heart on them to bless them – in much the same way as a person might determine to leave someone a fortune in his will. All the emphasis is on what God has decided to do.

66 The Lord said to Abram, 'Leave your native land, your relatives, and your father's home, and go to a country that I am going to show you. I will give you many descendants, and they will become a great nation. I will bless you and make your name famous, so that you will be a blessing.

'I will bless those who bless you, but I will curse those who curse you. And through you I will bless all the nations.'

When Abram was seventy-five years old, he started out from Haran, as the Lord had told him to do; and Lot went with him. Abram took his wife Sarai, his nephew Lot, and all the wealth and all the slaves they had acquired in Haran, and they started out for the land of Canaan. 99

Genesis, Chapter 12

THE STORY OF THE PEOPLE OF GOD

Ⓢ ome time around the year 1250BC, a rabble of Hebrew slaves escaped from the clutches of their Egyptian overlords.

Their leader was a man named Moses, an exiled prince of Egypt with Hebrew blood in his veins.

Moses

It was Moses' conviction that Yahweh, the Living God, was renewing his commitment to the Children of Israel, the Hebrews. He was demanding their release from slavery.

Not surprisingly, the ruling Pharoah, Ramesses II, was at first sceptical and then downright hostile. After all, he stood to lose the cheap labour which was building his treasure cities. Eventually he was obliged to give way because of a series of terrible plagues which were inflicted on the Egyptians by Moses' new-found God.   •

The last of these, and the one which finally changed Pharaoh's mind, was the sudden death of every firstborn child and animal in the land.

Passover

The night before they left Egypt, the Hebrews ate a final meal. They killed a lamb for every household and splashed its blood on the doorposts and lintels outside. This was a sign to God to 'pass over' the family and spare the firstborn. They then roasted the lamb and ate it quickly, with unleavened bread – there was no time to let the dough rise before baking it. Even as they ate, they had their bags packed and were dressed for the journey. By dawn they were on their way.

Exodus

They had scarcely gone any distance when they came to a stretch of open water known as the Sea of Reeds. This would have been an impossible obstacle, had not God miraculously intervened. He caused a strong east wind to dry the marsh, and the entire company was able to cross in safety.

Meanwhile, Pharaoh had already changed his mind, and Egyptian chariots were in hot pursuit. As they swept across the reed beds, the strong wind slackened and the water began to return. The chariot wheels became bogged down in the mud, and both horses and men were drowned.

To this day, the Jews look back to the Exodus (which means 'way out') as the birth of their nation. It was the point at which they realized their identity as God's people. Yahweh, the Living God, rescued them from bondage and despair and, against all the odds, gave them a present freedom and a future hope.

The seal of freedom

In due course, the Children of Israel were led to the slopes of Mount Sinai. Here God revealed himself in earthquake, fire and storm. He was awesome and unapproachable in his holiness. And yet he was on their side!

At Sinai, God bound himself to Israel in an everlasting covenant, and delivered to Moses his Law.

Strange as it may seem, the covenant of Sinai was not legalistic! It is true that at this point the Ten Commandments and other laws were given, but these were part of the privilege of belonging to God.

Israel did not earn her freedom by keeping the Law. The Law was given *after* deliverance from Egypt. It was intended to set a seal on their freedom and enable them to live full lives.

The Ten Commandments

The first four commandments relate to God.

1 'I am the Lord your God who brought you out of Egypt, where you were slaves. Worship no god but me.'
God establishes his identity as the one who delivered his people from Egypt. He alone is worthy of their worship.

2 'Do not make for yourselves images of anything in heaven or on earth or in the water under the earth . . .'
People are not to make images or idols of God. He is all-powerful and invisible. Any man-made idol, however well-intentioned, would not only appear to reduce him, but would be dumb, powerless, and easily dismissed.

3 'Do not use my name for evil purposes . . .'
God is holy, and his name (which includes his reputation) is to be treated with the utmost reverence. It is not to be used as a swear word, or as a guarantee on empty promises.

4 'Observe the Sabbath and keep it holy . . .'
One day in the week is to be kept as the Sabbath. It is a holy day, dedicated to God. It is a time for worship and rest – a taste of heaven.

The last six commandments relate to other people.

5 'Respect your father and your mother, so that you may live a long time in the land that I am giving you.' Parents and elders are to be respected. In this way family life will be strong, and the national life secure.

6 'Do not commit murder.' Human life is sacred.

7 'Do not commit adultery.' Marriage is an exclusive commitment between husband and wife, and must not be undermined by either partner having an affair.

8 'Do not steal.' A secret of stable community is respect for the property of others. This applies both to personal possessions and personal reputations.

9 'Do not accuse anyone falsely.' Speaking and living the truth is absolutely vital.

10 'Do not desire another man's house; do not desire his wife, his slaves, his cattle, his donkeys, or anything else that he owns.' Envy is the 'domino' which knocks over the other commandments. So the last commandment urges people to be content with what they have. Once envy is allowed to creep in, murder, adultery, theft and falsehood follow.

THE PROMISED LAND

After a generation of wandering around the wilderness of Sinai, the Children of Israel conquered the land of Canaan, under the leadership of Joshua. For some years they were led by Judges, of whom the most famous was the prophet Samuel. But as time went on, the people began to clamour for a king.

Samuel argued that God was the ruler of Israel, and that they didn't need a king like other nations. Eventually the pressure for a strong human leader was so great that God chose a tall, handsome and gifted young man, and Samuel anointed him. His name was Saul.

Saul

In fact, the reign of King Saul was a big disappointment. The pressures of leadership, coupled with disobedience to God and jealousy of the up-and-coming David, plunged him into bouts of depression. In the end, lonely and exhausted, he committed suicide during a battle with the Philistines.

David

It was under Saul's successor, King David (of Goliath fame!) that Israel